when You love some

when you Love someone
you never let them go
when you Love someone
you let It All show The
Planted seeds oF love you
Feed It;To grow when you
Love Someone you will
Just Know when you love
someone Theres no
GoodBye
IN real LiFe
And Love,
Theres No Bad guy Feelings oF
Love, yoU cANNoT Hide Because
when you love someone Its
pours from Inside. when you
love someone make sure that Its
me when you love someone
Make sure That Its free when
you Love someone DONT Bring
up the past
Theres Too Much, To Count
To Begin the math. Just
STArt Fresh when you love
someone at least, I can
Speak For Me when I Love,
Some one

DARK Nights

If you dont Know pain
Like I Know pain
IF you haven't Count Days
Like I counted Days,.. ----
No matter What I never Been afraid
Just look forward to Another way
and Better days Tears Drop, when I
remember
Dark Nights
IN A cell, Behind Doors,
I couldn't see Any light what can I say
It was a Hell of a fight
It Left scars On my heart
But I covered It right
Had Dark memories,
But I Buried them tight
People think that they strong
UnTill they locked, In chains
IF you don't walk In my shoes
You don't Know all my pain

erAse My PAiN

saw people In
and OUT
I wanted someone to cAre
WANted Someone to Be there
But NoBody Dares
Its so sad In real liFe makes
you want to shed Tears. I
didn't know, all the pressure
that came with facing _ Some
fears nightmare's of NO
Freedom Never Seeing my
Kids
I would pray every night
But It is what it is If I know
then what I Do know Now, ill
only change the pain that I
cause on my child I wish To
erase
All my days, Filed with Pain
I know things wont Be the same
But New beginning's, Bring
grace..

WAIK AWAY

you Came Here to Talk Bu
I have Noting to say
Please Turn around
Because you cannot stay
Im closing the doors I cant
open No more you Broke me
Down where I was already
ToRN Cant Believe What
you speak
Cant give In and Be weak
For you, I Been meek But
you couldn't, just see ..
don't make this Hard you
Played all your cards I
gave you my all which you
disregard WAIK away, DO
Not return what we Feel,
Let It Burn Im not trying
to be stern But A Lesson
I've learned...

Flames

Burning Inside
sometimes I cant Cry
emotions so deep I
Live on Both sides
Between heaven and earth
I Swear, I am Cursed Filled
wit memories. that Burn,
and they Hurt Flames on
my mind
Flames
In my Heart
Flames and more Flames
Im just Falling Apart why
do you Fake It
Just to then Take It all
the love gone
and No one, replaced It Flames
From my rage
Im Stuck In A cage
I Burn and I Burn No
turning the page. DONt
AsK me, what change
when all Is the Same Im
dying Inside
Because OF my Flames

Someday

maybe Someday Ill Spread my
wings and fly away Somehow, IN
my gaze maybe A-smile will
Appear Back on my face..
Someway, someday
Ill Live Life
Not caring
what others
may say For
my Sake,
Just Incase I'll
learn to accept
my Fate-..
Someone will Someday
Take this pain and Rage away
Someday
But Until that day
I'll be waiting lost
around. IN Some
place which I
dont Know
If I'll get out
of
Someday...

GOID TeARS

Pain After Struggle
Every-time I turn Pages
Through the Depression and anxiety
I was going trough stages -- left
without a mother When I needed
her most
But I couldn't change life
SO All I do, Is take Note
as time Goes By
I tAke pain like
A goat,
Keep my Head above water
more than
trying to float A Little
chapter of my Life
Now Im Closing the Book
Finally got my Freedom BAcK I
wont Forget what It tooK....
Gold Tears, that shine
Bright
My DARK Heart, Now enlightened
Thanking Gad for A chance
I Promise, to Never Stop Fighting

All Because OF You

Look me In my eyes
Never Forget my Look you
earned my Heart Never
Forget what It Took
whenever it rains
remember My Pain Thank
you my love For erasing
My stains when I tell you,
I-love you Better know;
That I mean It Its
the reason why,
every chance I get
 I Fill you with
Kisses
I cant seem To Forget you
DoNt ever search for another Because I
for sure, will never replace you ...
Memories that Are so Dark you came
Inside, and Brought some Light Im
Forever IN Debt, By your side, just hold
me tight...
IF at times, I Break and cry

Just Kiss my lips

DoNt Ask me why, somethings
In Life, I can't rewind
But having You, been Worth my time.
whenever I smile, Its only
Because of You who would of
ever knew Ill grow old only
To Love you
New Feelings you Bring me
Are hard to explain words
of your promises replay In
my Brain My Soul feels
WARm
Through all of Its storm
You came In my Like,
when I was All Torn you
made me be greatful ,
for the day you were
Born.

Me Or Her

you can Keep me close But
you cant have us Both
A Truth thats Never told
But time, It does
unfold... who owns your
Heart now ? who will It
Be then ? Will I end Up
as A Foe LoveR?
OR' Friend?
I Need to know
All The untold I Need
our love to Grow So
You'll Never Go .. ...
Me or Her?
who's more special to see me
oR Her? where would you
rather Be? Im Nothing like her
she can never be me, will she
Fill In my shoes OR will hers,
Be mine to Keep? BABy, tell
me Now lets cut the chase
avoid all the pain Of
A HeartBreak

so UnFaiR

so unfaiR ya
want to share so
UnfaiR Your
never there
In Your eyes
I always Stare
And IN my Heart
I seek repair
LiFe, LiFe So UnfaiR
I look around But
No one cares my
Heart, my Heart IN
Such, Despair
Reach ForYOU
But Its all clear Thats
life unfair Since, you're
Not Here....

I smile Again

because of you I Smile again The
one who cares and Never
pretends My BABY, my lover my
Dearest Friend I Promise, I'll stay
Beyond an end
Thanks to you I
smile again when I
was down you
spared A hand
YoU LifT me up
Above the sand I owe
you foR LiFe Since
way Back then..
Love you forever
Because I CAN,
and do It all over
and over, again ...

you failed me, like the rest
where I Believed in you most
I know no one is perfect
But, I thought with you, I had
Hope you lied to me and
For that,
I   wont
ever
Forgive
I won't allow you to think
That for one second,
It's cool what you did
I Never thought love can hurt,
Way worse than Hate
I Never Knew that
you would cross me
The first chance, you can take
 I Trusted you, Beyond my Insecurities
 I believed your lies, Beyond reality
Its crazy haw you tried to play me
and Lost morality I knew you was
up to something
I couldn't Put my finger ON It
I Asked you
Just Incase,   I was
tripping   when   all
Along,   you've Be my
opponent

SometimeS

Sometimes I wAnnA give up
Sometimes I wanna hold oN
Sometimes, I sit And replay out the
lies that you say But I choose to
think that sometimes
Is
oKay Sometimes you Break my
Heart
Sometimes you Tear It apart
Other times you Stitch It Together But
the pain, Still Is sharp..
Sometimes you say that you love me
Sometimes you Say that you miss me
But Its all so confusing , Because
you turn and just diss me..
Sometimes I wish I Never met you
sometimes I wish to forget you all
the love that I gave you It just
makes me, regret You - Sometimes
I close my Mind and ignore
sometimes I know your Not sure
It Kills me to Know that my love Is
all-yours I want to Be Numb
,because my LiFe IS ALL Sore.

Biting My Lips

Just how you imagined it
I'm Biting my Lips
Even from many miles away
Ill Always fine For a Kiss
Biting ON my Lips
Thinking of your touch
Thinking OF pleasure
Thinking of So much
Biting my Soft lips Picturing
You, Here with me diving In
my ocean, drowning Deep
Beneath my sea
Biting on my Lips
Just Dreaming About A Taste All
the Feelings that you bring me
and all the Sounds That you make
Biting on my Lips wishing they
can Be yours Imagining
Your Body
Exploring it
Like A tour
BitingON my Lips
Feeling Moist Between my Legs
Temperature rising in my sheets And
Thoughts Racing In my head.

Air balloon

AIR BallOON
Im up In the sty
Flying with theBirds
Forgetting the moment
regretting my words IF
I can go BAcK
Ill Fix what I Broke Ill take
you with me wherever I go
Im up In the sky like A
BallooN Filled with AiR
reliving the times, when you
always cared I wont Be
Coming Down
At least, No time soon
DONt WANt tO Feel
A HeartBreak
 At NOON
Fly away , with me
IF you should But I
want to Be Alone
thats really my mood

Free me Inside

locked In these chains Let
me Feel that Im Free
NoT Being Able to See Tomorrow
Let me know , you got me
God open my heart,
So
I can love with your Love and
clear my mind SO I can See
all your thoughts Free me
from the Borders that
Bury me so deep
Lift the weight off my shoulder
That Are heavy on my mind
Free me Deep within
No matter what I may Be Facing
Let   me   Look
Forward tO A Smile
maybe   even   A
HAppy ending
Free me LORD, Because I Cant
go ON my Problems growing
greater and my demons,
stand Strong. Free me lord
please
Give me Just one more chance
This worlds been so
Cold to me
It goes, so Fast, Im
In a trance.

SalT AND Pepper

Together, we go
Like salt ANd Pepper As
wAter andMud through
Stormy Weather HAND
INHAND
we walk through Life, Stuck
Together
Like DiNO-mites
Hold me In your arms
Until the end OF time,
Ill embrace you In mine
AND As Usual We will
shine.
Salt anD pepper
Peanut and Butter our
Lave Is BoNDed up
Like NO Other.

BAcK In Time

If only back Into Time
I can maybe rewind I would of
Never Hurt you your the only,
one, On my mind If I can go
Back to Yesterday
I would of Never let you Go I
would of ony let you know That
I Need you there to grow ... IF I
Can go BAcK In time
I word say only whats needed I
would've opened my Mind so that
myHeart, you have greeted But I
shut you off
I Broke you down
I Drained you for your lire
And i Let you down
If I can go Back In time I would
kiss you, one more time.
I would release all this pain
That I Keep deep Inside

Giving up Now

I Tried, I-tried
And you know this
You wounds and pain
I healed, with a Kiss you
Broke me, you Broke me
OH, Thats so
Sad Im giving up Now Dont
know, why, you would ask...
There nothing Here, left for me
we took things so ungreatfully
could of Done It differently Now,
Im Running Drastically..
Away From you Away From Love
No Need to Search, Because
Im gone
I knew it was Done,
In the long run But I choose to
chance It, all along was HaRD with
the world, But Turned soft For
you, crazy How life's unfaiR and
switches out the Blue..
Now
At me you laugh
Im so ashamed
Because I Never realized
Love been left me, Before
It even ever Came..

when It Rains

Im Broken hearted My
emotions scattered
screaming For healing
got My dreams Shattered
cold and lonely Numb
and Insane, those are
my feelings whenever It
rains The thunder
Is my Anger The Drops, are
my tears The wind Is really
me AloNe, with No-one
near. Pain, wash away
Please go with the mud, all
oF my scars and secret's
Lets sweep under the Rug ...
When It rains I
cry, and when I
cry, I die Deep
down Inside.
My Tears, Like
Rain cause a
flood Like a
little child
Im In Need of hugs

I remember

I remember days
Use To Feel like A year
I remember Taking losses But
I couldn't shed Tears -.
I remember your love
Dont remember when
It died
I remember when LiFe gave
Up   ON   me,   Inside.   I
remember your voice   the
days you would call me I
remember how   persistent
you was to comFront me I
remember you Fought
 For all of my love Now,
when I need you the most
Your shoulders Just shrug ...
I remember the pain
That came, when It rained
 I remember when my Smile
WAS tooKen IN vain I
Remember Being alone
with No one to call
I remember going through the mud
But somehow, wont Fall -
I remember To my cries
No one wound answer I
remember closing my eyes
wishing time Can go
Faster
I remember So much BAD,
I can't recall All the good
I remember, all My trying
But yet, was always, misunderstood

RainBow

The colors of the rainbow Every Color,
- different aura different Mood, ,
different you. Beautiful, ugly, what
color defines you?
red, orange, fellow , green, Beige
, purple de indigo?
After the rain
- Comes sun Then a
beautiful rainbow
Pot OF Gold waiting at the end?
Little green Iris men?
A sign of peace , A sign of Love
 A Sign That God, Is with
 US
After heavy rain Droplets 7
BeautiFUl Colors, Full of meaning
and Ugly human
Beings.

Pinky Promise

"I love you" you Said
so I gave you all of me
Together forever
,A Pinky Promise
I let all of me let go
In your presence Just to
Be let down the
happiness drifts the
hopelessness sinks gave
you all of me , Still wasn't
enough Mania and
sadness diagnosed
disorders all Because of
you was doing so well,
Just for It to go downHill
dawn Into a wishing Well,
But except
NO Wish Was
granted.

Remote

wired to Be controlled Full of
demands Your voice the
Remote that controls me
reassures me Ad well as
hurts me
Im a Robot, your the master
Silver and complicated Buttons A
genie That grants all your wishes
what Am i to you ,all Rolled in one
wires cut,A slave NO more Im free
But your time has just begun I'm
no longer
A remote
So your no longer
In
Control

Math class

I added up what you did
I even subtracted, what U said I
did the mate all In my head and
It still DoNt make no sense I
thought I was Dumb
Thought I was overthinking
But I was wrong
 I was Right all along,
Welcome to math class
Stuck In long equations,
Still can't do division
The Favorite subject
Your a master at

ScaRecrows

Look at the little scarecrow
Scaring the crows away Chooo
!!chooo cho!!!
Protected me , made me feel special
For as FAR as fear
I remember
But In the end all you did, was scare me away
Lost my
Respect, , Lost my trust
Lost my
Lover
Lost It All
Hope it was worth It
Look at you now
Little
Scare crow

Lioness

all BARK, All Bite the
cowardly   Lion   No
courage,   to make me
yours Your Not Brave
enough
No man enough
Just an Immature little Boy
FULL of anger and throws
It at the world
All bark all bite
But Also all Coward will
never Be a man, will
Never   learn   You'll
Forever, Be alone
A coward
Till the end
Who can't no longer Have
lioness!

Suicide

overdose,neck hanging So many
different ways to die so many
different ways to end it all Is life
really It? Is It all that It Is? great
highs,painful lows
Read the note
Suicide
No more pain
Ceasefire tears, Finally clean
At peace in the clouds
Where I'm meant to be
Empty, feeling no more
Pinch me I won't bleed
Hit me I won't feel
This time it's me Time
to leave .

Peterman

All fun No responsibilities running
away from a dark place up,down
around and around Neverland
Laughing with PetterPan
Flying ,I'm tinker-bell
Back and forth
From never land
Amazing things I saw
And told
Amazing things
Are safe untold
Me in the sky with PeterPan
Is way better than waking up
Again, in never-land
Loyalty greater than love
Love greater than pain tell
me those things aren't
starting To sound the
same ?
Never land never land
Gives me what peterPan can't So,So
we'll ,to my dear
 oldest friend ,PeterPan

Part two
Hurricane Love

The Freaky Things

Every thing that we
do Is freaky you
make me drip
So sticky ....
Just your voice
alone Does It, to me
SeX BAcK TO BACK
Leave me hickeys.
How you do this
How you de That
How you Keep me hooked
Just LiKe Crook . From the
BAcK of from the front The
Freaky things
All At Once
Cant get enough
I need Everyday
the way you give It
to me
I Cant help
 But Stay

Beautiful Curves

Walking towards you
I see the Lust on your face
Fieing For your love
I don't Mind you to stay
delicious Curves, My Body
All yours Lets make wild love
and Burn out our pours... I
Need your hands on me
,your eyes on Mine your
Kisses oN my Neck and
Some Down my Spine .... Is
wish you inside wit NO Limits
 Between US
Rocking my world
Rebuilding my trust
Sex so sweet
Its SimilAR
To honey
Ima Rock with you
Therefore
Ill Never Be lonely

Its Simple to you

so easy for you To
tell me to chill
Its Simple For you
To Do, what you will
But , for me
Its difficult
To Suppress what I Feel
Promise I want to Be numb
and my emotions, all kill Its
simple for you
To Not, understand Because
your Not In my shoes and
stand where I stand... easy
Breezy, all so Simple IF only,I
cAN relate
All that for love You
speak on must Be
Fake- .. This Is the
hardest thing
I believe
I've ever done realizing
how Its Simple For you
To Let me Just
 RUN...

Let me Go

just let me Go If you
truly love Another
Please walk
Away Now
Don't make my heart shatter Don't
Be Selfish,
If you know you cant love me
Don't pretend that Im Her
when Its her that you See
You Go Your wAy And I'll Go
mine woNt think of the Days
You made It All Shine I Got
To Run, Got To Protect my
world from Destruction
Concerned my Heart Is weak
Wounded, under construction....
I love you Always
But ill Do It from AFAR
I cAnt Afford you, Right NoW
Leaving more SCARS...

- your embrace

you Been gone all day
and I really miss your Face
Can you hurry Back home
Because Im Needing your embrace.
Feeling lonely at home
Lets watch Netflix and chill
Please, pick up the phone Need your
voice, Just To heal as I miss your smile
and your touch Baby, I miss your hugs and
all your Love ...
Spare me my tears and cause me to Smile
Put a ring-on my finger
Lets creat US A child
your embrace Is so sweet
Its all that I need,
through thick and the thin
You're the air that I
breath

Through The mud, and the rain

with our love put Together
we can get through whatever
our energies are great But
there greater together.
rescued me from the mud
that came From the rain
Helped me heal my Heart
that was sinking Ih pain Cant
say Im NoT lucky
By far, Im the luckiest Just to have
you In My life won't have to go
through the ugliest
we are a team Build OF Two
Souls , where would I Be
without you
NOT even GoD knows
Ill always give Strength
If your ever Feeling weaK,
Because I Knows With NO dought
You'd Do the same for me

YOU ARE

you are lovable, I love you you
are Beautiful, ill Flaunt you so
Intelligent, Ill learn From you
you are sexy,I'll experience you
amazingly delicious ,Taste you
Tenderly sort, I cuddle wit you
You are an asset, Ill invest In you
Undoubtedly earning full, Ill cherish you
when your sensitive, Ill Comfort you You
are priceless, ill value you You are my
diamond ,I'll reflect on you you are
radiant, Ill Bask In you yo are too strong,
Ill gain strength for you you are deep ,I'll
seek To understand you you are striking,
I stand In awe of you you are, all that, I'm
Impressed By you You are Funny, I laugh
with you you are giving, so I share with
you Very spiritual, Ill pray with you You
are Forgiving, so Ill Forgive you your my
everything, you are my reason
You are who I Love Im
IN love with you And,
who you are.

Real Love Is LiKe.

Like Taking a walk In a park on
a Beautiful summer day Like
relaxing By the Bay as IF
everything okay... real love Is
unbelievable so reliable and
unconditional real love Is, like
forever real love Is, Never
Seasonal.
Looking Into your soul
I Find real Love
Searching Into our Lives
I recall real hugs
Don't know what Hate Is like with
your real love around, embracing,
My Heart, Filed with Joy Love that
makes me feel Found..
In Need Of A solution
I seek quickly For your Security Never
Fearing problems with you, I overcome
them with Integrity Thanks to you, love
Its Been Like, riding A Bike,
Thanks to you BaBy
I know what love Is like

Will you stay

By my side, will you stay
Without any complaints if
If hurt you by mistake Will
you still here remain?
That's what you did
And I still want you near So
will you stay baby?
I need you right here
When you lied to me
You knew what to say
I never wanted you away
So tell me you'll stay

Toxic

Used to be toxic
In love with the bitter Sweet
I don't want to move on Forget,
or retreat
I love you even when
You don't love me
Hooked on the falls Can't
cope with the real
I'll deal with the ugly
As long as you near

Christmas with you

Every day by your side It's like
spending Christmas with you Loving
you so much It's some thing I didn't
know how to do
Slowly, I became a pro
At letting my love show
Sadness doesn't live here
At least not anymore
Life with you as a holiday
In each and every way
I swear, feels like Christmas
Each and every day
Love with no limits
Oh, for my ride or die
With love, a strong as yours Love
here will never fly
I'd rather be here
Every day is amazing with you
Because, like I said, I already
Love will always be Christmas with you

You and I

You and
Real love, real life
It's so amazing
That you and I realize
What hides behind the truth
Is sometimes real lies
But things are all true
When it comes to you and I
I can't be right here
Or 1,000,000 miles across
Either way, our love is felt
And can never be lost
You and I
Need nothing else
Me and you
In our shell
Forever and ever
I love you
Today yesterday
And tomorrow
It's me and you

Honeymoon

Imagine our honeymoon , perfect
something unseen, where we will
share our love together with nothing
coming in between watching the
waves clap at sunset watch the sun
go down can't wait until this
honeymoon finally comes around.
Let's play on the rooftops and
make wishes upon stars let's
allow our love to take off And go
up all the way to Mars
something beautiful coming alive
it's what our love will be like
sewing for lifetime and finally
getting
To reap
Baby, I love you
I'm waiting on the day to come soon
I'm already planning our wedding
And won't forget The
    honeymoon

Butterfly

Butterfly butterfly
Living the truth, through the lies
Butterfly seems so numb
Flying smooth through the skies
Dreams of one day flying away Up
high with a butterfly That day can't
come fast by the way
I'm dying inside
Butterfly dearest friend
Who never makes me cry
Beautiful you that passes by
But never tells me lies
Maybe someday someway You
can stay
Flying in my heart
Erasing my days
And healing my pain
Butterfly butterfly
A master of disguise
Who goes around the world
And never seems surprised

Instead

Again my friend You can
tell that I'm broken Look
into my eyes You'll see
that I'm choking From all
the grief
That within me I'm holding
Can't seem to pull through So
after all o keep folding Bury
me alive
Because I'm ugly inside
I live through my days
As if they were my nights Alone
in my bed
All in my head
Tears that keep falling
No smiles are Instead

Demons

Shadows that at night
Hold my hand
 Decisions that are hard
Made By man my
Sanity I SweAR
Im trying to keep
But It gets harder And
harder as heart aches
repeat   when I caNt
speAK my Anger just
screams My Demons
just wIN as I go
through somethings
Afraid OF rejection
receiving Neglection
Taming my Beast
For my own Protection
Seeking the day I may
Live again for Now it's
my Demons that Dont
seek a Friend.

Mood swings

I can be up The next
minute I'm down
You choose to be there And
then not around
I'm and out
Round and round
So unstable
To stand my ground
The unspoken The
unseen And all that's
between Keeps me
all alone With no one
to lean
I'm happy
Then I'm mad
So many mood swings
Don't know what I feel
Can't locate what is real My
joy it just steals
I believe
Then I doubt
I cry
Then u shout Tell
me what do I do
Tell me what it's about !?

Happy V Day

Thank you for your love
Here are Some roses Thank
you for your years and
Never Loosing Focus Thank
you, for Staying loyal
 Here are some chocolates
Thank you, for remaining humble
Here are my Promises
1
Love you Forever 2 stay
through any weather 3 meet
you half way where-ever
4
put a smile on your face everyday
5
Put A ring on Your finger Someday
6
Protect you always happy valentines day
My sweet heart
Im thankful for you,
Just Keep doing Your part

Come here

Come here
And love me more
Hold my hand
And let it show
I'm my heart
Your kept safe
Loving you forever
With no other way
Come here
Kiss my lips
Pull me closer
And grip my hips
Come here Don't
run away
A love like mine
Will be no other place
Come here
And lay with me
If your not near
I cannot breath
Our souls are tied And
we know why
Our love so high
It touched the sky Come
here
 let's tie the knot In
your mind and heart
Are my favorite spots Come
here
Please don't wait
Let's make today
The best of days
I'll meet you here
So we can share
Where ever you go
I'll be right there

When I say I love you

When you say I love you
Say it because you mean it
When you look into my eyes
Can you hear my heart beating
I get lost loose my breath
Gain the world in a minute
I don't care what is wrong
Because I'm alright If your in it
When you say I love you
I need to feel the words
So that I can always remember
When we go through the worst When
I say I love you
It's all from my heart
You're the stitches
That keep it together
From falling apart
When you say I love you
It heals my wounds
Just those emotions from you
Always make me new
I never want to go
I need that I love you
Because if I wake
And your not here
I'll need to die soon

Im from the bottom

What can I say
I'm so tired of things
Things to Bargain with the devil
But I'm tied to some strings
I know myself
Therefore I'll never switch
Running through the streets
Until they make me rich
All evil they speak on me
It gives me a kick
Wouldn't care if you hate me
It is what it is   ain't No
Secrets In this game It was
always told what you want to
do Because I can get
I'm that mood
I like to smile
But whats Inside ,
 I do Not show Trust me
when I say   you DoNt
want No issues I grew up
at the Bottom
My shoes were never Brand new
I share No pity, I never Feel
remorse. I have No
Sympathy For someone,
who Is worse. who's colder
than me you are, By all
means - But DoNt get
blinded to underestimate
whats unsaid, thats In
Between...

What is love

The arms of safety,
words of love
Acts of service ,genuine laughter Is
that it ? Is that love ? What is love?
Thought I knew
Movies and tv shows ,teenage love
A painful thing
Reality is not tv
Before any love comes pain
No definition no meaning
Still no clue still no idea
Tell me ,what is love
Show me ,what is love
I love love and it's purity

It wants what it wants

Not stupid not dumb just in love
Wrong or right , right or wrong
The heart want what it wants
Regardless what my head says
How my heart beats
Beats how my mind thinks
Bad for me ,right for me
I can't see , or can I ? and I can't let go
My body wants you
My heart beats for you
Boys coming both ways ,great and bigger
But my heart wants what it wants

Within me

My roots deep in the ground
Always with me like the moon and it's light
The sun and it's shine
When the rain is pouring
Watch the flowers start growing
No rain no flowers the rain and it's powers
My roots grow deeper than deep
Always with me my nature my scene
The heart that beats inside me
Thank you thank me
As your love grows always
Within me

Chess

Pawns ,knights, and queens
Which one am I in your game
Blinded ,couldn't see ,you were different than me
So I thought
Seen the lights ,saw the truth
Now anger is all in my view
I was your pawn and you my king
How stupid
Can I be
Caught in your web
Listened to your words
Only to be a fool in the end
Our world was a game of chess
And your
The best
Player

Over the cliff

I'm over the cliff
I want to jump off
I'm dealing with things
That have been too tough
I'm through with the games
I'm tying the knot
To avoid any more pain
And my heart to just stop
I'm over the cliff
I'm dangling from the edge
I'm crying to sleep
Alone in my head
I wake up to nightmares
There's sweat on my bed
I'm replaying the things
That make me feel dead
If I jump
Please don't safe me
I'm numb to pain
That raised me over the cliff
I'm fed up
There's no point of trying
When I'm all out of luck

What you Took

How dare you try to give Back what
you Took
You stole then Broke my Heart what A crook...
I DoNt want It Now
Its all damaged Goods
Keep It, and see what Its worth
IF, you could what you toOK
Its Innocence that makes you guilty
For Destroying A girl That use
to Be pretty why didn't, you
take the pain why didn't, you
Take the blame sad, you
preyed on me for you should
Be ashamed... What you took
Has Not worth without
Consent you just searched
Now my heart
Needs' A Nurse,
 It was Bad,
 Now, Its worse.

Time heals

They say time heals all
I heard someone mention
But can it heal scars
That left me ,all this tension
I plan to hop in my car
And keep aiming for the stars.
Once time does its course
All this pain disregards
Maybe time can heal my soul
Like a good written poetry
Or even make a new heart
Like its doing surgery
I need time to heal me
Until this pain just stops
Keep working over time
Until I run out the clock

Rain drops

Rain drops rain drops
Wash away all my pain
Rain drops keep falling
Down my eyes anyways
Rain drops so small
Can carry so much weight
Rain drops at night
And rain drops at day
Wishing these drops an heal
All my tears that fall stray
Why does my mind betray
What my heart feels its okay
Why do rain drops keep pouring
Where my head always lays
Wetting the pillow wetting the bed
Rain drops rain drops
Keep drowning my head
When will the sun dry my rain drops
When will the sun
Dry up my stains
Left by all the pain
That caused my eyes
To constantly rain.

What you Took

I close my eyes
I see you
you watch me,
Im see through
I cry all the time
and don't know why
Its so hard,
Why Love dies?
I try to forgive you
Because Indeed
your all I ever Need
And Your all I ever see...
can forget what was done
What made Love under the sun
But still In the end, Nobody won
And now I'm missing you for the long run
Yet you follow me I still feel your kisses
I'm still respecting your wishes
See your face like glitches
I love you but I hate you
you changed and I don't know why
I did all to protect you
But you took me for granted
It's fuck you

Plenty Faces

show me one Face
give the world another
 Act like were just friends
But selling dreams of lovers ...
Smile In one face
But Stab Behind another
How many faces Do you have
that are made of Rubber.
you say one thing
But Don't really mean It
you say you love me
I Don't really see It
so many Places
Looking at Plenty faces
going through stages
where everything changes
You Talk about me;
you say you don't understand
why I'm so Broken, Guess your Blind
Look again.

Someone

I Need Someone to hold
and Not For making love
Someone to make me feel needed
Someone to feel Part of
This feeling so heavy
my Heart Is Broken I
Need to Be held
without any word Spoken .
Someone to Be right here
Someone will wipe my Tears
Help me face my fears
And WONt Be AFraid To Stay NeAR
I want Someone to Kiss
But Noting More
Someono to share affection
 and accept my imperfections
I Ned you to see
that Together well feel free
Someono who Can Be
all youll ever need

Today is a new day

Yesterday was yesterday
Todays A newday,
Tomorrow's not promised
Lets just See what It makes...
Decisions To ponder on,
choices To make,
The world gives and takes
But Its all for our sake ...
If we wake
Its never too late
To rejoice and partake,
In all the mercy and favor,
that No one can fake
Full oF greatness Inside,
Lets Not give It away
Come on, Lets Together Celebrate
that Tadays A new day.

gray world

Trying to tame my Beast
Trying to leave them Streets
Trying to Let Go,
And Be free
But, I just cant Be
Someone So Beautiful made
But the moments won't Fade
so equally Damaged
I'm this world full of shade
In a world full of Strays
that Never Found a way
Ima close the curtains
Im making A Vow
 that what Im Feeling Right Now
Is just A Dark Cloud
maybe Just
For today
maybe
Just For always
But atleast Im greatful to Say
That everyday I can-try again

Dark Road

I want to quit
But I Keep going
Wanna Stop ,But Keep ON Pouring
my skies are gray, Its always Storming
my Soul Is cold,
my Heart Is snowing
Everyplace I turn A DOOR Is closing
Every time i trust I feel exposed
Alive to myself
But dead to most
But Its my fault
Its what I choose
To wear my memories,
as dirty clothes
I drop my tears,
To show my Fears
I wish you Near,
so I wont steer
down A Dark Road,
that's never Clear
Clouded with emotions,
Like IF , Drunk OFF Beer
Steady trying to make real, what Is False
Steady trying hard, Steady Taking A Loss
All my regrets, I'm trying wash
all my pain
That Drips Like Sauce

Which one is it

What is it that you want to do?
Where do you want to go?
Which one is it I don't know
The way you're going we won't grow.
Pain pain that won't go away.
Tears of emotions that won't fade.
Tribulations that I made.
It's all my fault guess I played.
I thought I was ready.
For too long I was empty
Dealing with issues that made me.
And karma that paid me
Which one is it that you seek
Happiness sadness maybe meek
I'm in and out, I'm down the street.
Tell me what you want.
At least with me

Sadness

At night I cry in silence
Mind in autopilot
Emotions overflowing
I'm in tears I'm drowning
Sorrow is what I feel
My hopes they always steal
My dreams somebody killed
Now my sadness overfill
Things that don't add up
Makes no sense it had me stuck
Thinking of a way I'd find some luck
But crash into a wall my feelings tuck
Sadness hurts breaks me down
Smiles fade away since your not around
I cry And I cry but make no sounds
I lost my smile so I just frown

Filled with rage

Fire in my eyes
Darkness in my soul
Flames fill me up
Pain that makes me fold
Fed all the way up
Mad at evryone just because
Life hasn't been fair
And all the secrets of lust
How dare you try
To stand up to me
I'm dangerously filled with rage
You're a fool to disagree
Done come near
Stop trying to make me feel
don't compare
Because I'm made of steel

Upset

Outraged I'm upset
I feel they owe me soemthing
Give me back my joy
Let me spread my wings
I can't believe
I feel this way
I won't achieve
Another day
I want to let loose
And burst in rage
I don't want to be mad
But I can't help feel this way
I think I need therapy
Maybe someone to speak to
Someone who will listen
And not try to see through
I'm afraid I'm upset
What more can I say
I'm mad at the world
For what I'm living today

Hold me

Embrace me my love
Hold me real tight
The lord is my light
And you are my knight
Keep me when I'm scared
Promise me to be there
Hold me in your arms
And forever keep me there
Don't let me go
Don't ever leave
Hold me baby please
Without you I can't breath
Your eyes tell me truth
Your words confirm your love
Your love keeps me awake
Your actions give me hugs
For today hold me safe
For today hold me safe
For tomorrow guide my heart
And the next keep me sane
Until forever never part

I'm no enemy

From different paths of life
We are all different and special
I'm not here to judge you
I'm not out to get you
I stand firm like a statue
And you
You just live what they taught you
Love feels great
But hate is so strong
Tell me what did I do ?
To make you feel harm ?

I made it

I use to be unsure
Look at me now
I was once torn and broken
And now I just smile
No more need for pain
No more being the same
When the live for myself
Finally stepped up and came
I made it at last
I did it for me
I'm finally the one
People said I couldn't be
I carry my own
I fixed my own crown
I'm no longer so weak
Now I stand firm on the ground
Making myself proud
Knowing I made it
Never lost now
Just glad I can say it

You can have it all

What I feel
You can have it
The idea of love
I just grasp it
All that I think of
Is you
I'd give you the world
And what is new
I love you
With my heart
I need you
With my soul
I won't leave
I won't betray you
Even if I'm forced to go
My lover my baby
The reason I smile
My hero
My strength
The number to dial

Sorrow

In search of destiny
I'll always need tomorrow
There's no need to. Rush
For tomorrow time ,is borrowed
Tomorrow's time is never promised
But to someone
There will always be a tomorrow
Even if I'm gone
Then tomorrow will bring sorrow
Feeling sadness
I cannot hide
Yet I live on
And I sacrifice
Another moment
Another way
To change my feelings
And saddest days

There's always tomorrow

There's always tomorrow
Where there's a way
There's always my hope
That day can be great
Waiting for tomorrow
I'm case today brings misery
Can't wait to wake tomorrow
And find out it's mystery
Today the sun shines
But tomorrow is untold
That's whats different about today
That tomorrow is unknown

No man

No man provides love
No man provides me shelter
No man is greater than another
And specially not the father
Perfect love perfect vision
Perfect comfort perfect mission
If o Lu we would take the time to listen
Realize he's the king our lives been missing
No man can compare to my father
No land to his kingdom
No one knows or will have his wisdom

Lost child

Poor lost child
That didn't know love
That use to be me
Who needed a hug
To fend for myself
Me against the world
To fight the battle of life
Just being a girl
Coming from nothing
I grew up to something
I never gave up
For a chance I kept hunting
Was a lost child
But I became found
I owe to myself
The most beautiful crown
Living out struggle
Loving through pain
Forgiving my past
overcoming my shame

Only the family

Only the family
Will always be there
Only the family
Will truly much care
Through fights and bad moments
We will always survive
Because only the family
In the heart will reside
When you speak on trust
Tell me who you see
I know it cannot be a random
It's only the family
Not perfect but amazing
All together breathtaking
Family who sticks together
Family who stands forever
That is truly embracing

A father I saw

A Father's I saw
Has no limits
A Father's I saw,
is never timid
Some fathers I saw
Never made it
Some fathers just stall
And are truly hated
My father, I knew
Waste the time
The father I loved
For sure wasn't mine
The father I needed
Wasn't there
A fatherless child
You couldn't compare
The father I made
So glad he is great
The father I saw
Is my husband today

The end .

Made in the USA
Columbia, SC
02 October 2023

23635567R00046